Intro
B109.
Characterisation of Pieces.
Evaluation.

THE PRECES PRIVATAE

THE
PRECES PRIVATAE
OF
LANCELOT ANDREWES
BISHOP OF WINCHESTER

TRANSLATED

WITH AN INTRODUCTION AND NOTES

BY

F. E. BRIGHTMAN, M.A.

FELLOW OF S. MARY MAGDALEN COLLEGE, OXFORD

CANON OF LINCOLN

METHUEN & CO.

36 ESSEX STREET W.C.

LONDON

1903

PREFACE

A DESCRIPTION of the character of the present volume will perhaps at the same time serve as an excuse for a new version of an old and famous book.

1. The text which has been translated is that of the Oxford edition of 1675, corrected and supplemented by the MSS., especially the Laudian MS., which contains a considerable mass of Hebrew matter that was not represented in the edition of 1675, and the Harleian MS., the contents of which are almost wholly outside the scope of the edition of 1675 and have never as a whole appeared in English. To this is added the matter recovered from Stokes' *Verus Christianus*, which, while in many cases it represents only a preliminary form of what is contained in the other sources, yet includes some new passages, and throughout offers points of interest which seem worth preserving. The sources of the text are indicated in detail on the inner margin.[1]

2. In the translation the aim has been, where the original is drawn from the Septuagint or the Vulgate, to use the language of the Authorised Version and of the Psalter of the Book of Common Prayer, except in cases in which for any reason correction seemed necessary or desirable, or Andrewes elsewhere supplies a corrected rendering of his own. Where the text of the Septuagint or the Vulgate is altered, some attempt has been made to represent this in the English ; but it has proved scarcely possible to carry out this plan consistently, and perhaps it was not worth while to attempt it in detail. Where the original text is quotation from the Hebrew of the Old Testament, the rendering of the Authorised Version has been corrected, largely in the direction of the Revised Version of 1881. Outside of quotations from Holy Scripture, the translation has been

---

[1] As a rule only the *ultimate* source is indicated ; but it must be remembered that all that is in W and W is also in O.

made anew and the text adhered to as nearly as possible. But regard has been had to Andrewes' own rendering of such passages as occur elsewhere in his writings and to the language of the *Sermons* generally. Apart from this the influence of Cardinal Newman and Dr Neale will be obvious. No one who has made much use of their version will be either able or willing to ignore it. Very rarely a few words have been added to ease or complete the sense ; and these are enclosed in pointed brackets.

3. The whole book has been rearranged for practical use, and redistributed, as far as possible in accordance with the Bishop's own scheme of devotion as given on pp. 12 sq. In the edition of 1675 and in versions dependent on it, the contents of the ' second part ' are not only kept quite distinct from those of the first, but are wholly without arrangement : it would seem that Andrews' papers were printed without any attempt to put them in order, with the result that this part of the *Preces* has probably been little used as a whole. It is sometimes difficult to know exactly where to put a paragraph or fragment, but it may be hoped that the present arrangement will serve practical purposes. For titles, etc., which are printed in thick type and mark the arrangement of the text, I am responsible. The Greek MSS. have no titles, and those of the ' second part' are incomplete and un-systematic ; and for the titles in former versions the editors have been mostly responsible.

4. Where the original is in Hebrew, the translation is printed in italic [1]; but no attempt has been made to mark the distinction between the Greek and the Latin of the original.

5. With regard to the arrangement of the lines of the text, the Laudian MS. has been taken as authoritative, and over the ground covered by its contents, its arrange-ment has been as far as possible almost exactly followed. Elsewhere, the arrangement of the current text has not been regarded as finally authoritative, but while it has been adhered to in general, it has been modified in detail in accordance with what seem to be the principles of the Laudian MS., and occasionally in accordance with mere

---

[1] *i.e.* everything printed in Italic represents Hebrew in the original, with the exception of the sub-titles on pp. 171-177.

convenience. The Hebrew of the Laudian MS. is not arranged like the Greek, but in general all the lines begin at the same level. Where a given passage is only in Hebrew this arrangement has been reproduced ; but where the parallel Greek is added, this is indicated by the arrangement of the italic text in accordance with the Greek.

6. References to sources are added in the outer margin. The Scriptural references of course apply to the text of the original, and consequently they may not always be recognisable in the English Bible. But when the difference is a marked one, ' heb.,' ' sept.,' or ' vulg.' is commonly added to the reference. When the original is only in Hebrew the reference is printed in italic ; but when the Greek is added, the reference is in ordinary type. An asterisk in the text indicates the end of the quotation ; where no such indication is given, it must be understood that the reference applies to the whole of the text down to the end of the paragraph or to the next marginal reference. In a few cases a quotation from Holy Scripture occurring within a quotation from some other source is indicated by a subordinate reference enclosed in square brackets. A note of interrogation in the margin indicates that a passage appears to be a quotation, but its source has not been discovered. The books and editions indicated in the nonscriptural references are given in the index ; but it may be well to repeat here that the Greek Liturgies (S. James, S. Basil, S. Chrysostom) are referred to in the edition used by Andrewes, printed by Morel at Paris in 1560 ; that ' Horae' represents the Sarum Horae printed at Paris in 1514, and ' Prymer' (without added date or publisher) represents the Sarum Prymer printed by Nicholas le Roux at Paris in 1537 ; and ' Heb. morn.,' ' Heb. even.,' etc., refer to the Synagogue morning and evening prayers, etc., as contained in The Authorised Daily Prayer Book of the United Hebrew Congregations of the British Empire, edited by the Rev. S. Singer, London, 1895.

7. The Notes are chiefly concerned with illustrating and explaining the text by the help of the other works of Andrewes, and treating the sources more fully than is possible in the margin. But some attempt at further exposition has been made where it seemed necessary, and occasionally an extended note has been written on the

origin and history of a topic or formula, where no convenient
reference could be given to its treatment elsewhere, or it
seemed possible to add anything to current accounts of
things. Both in the Notes and in the Introduction,
Andrewes' works are referred to as they are contained in
the *Library of Anglo-Catholic Theology*, except in the case
of the S. Pauls' and S. Giles' Lectures, which are referred
to in ΑΠΟΣΠΑΣΜΑΤΙΑ *sacra*, London, 1657.

It remains to return my best thanks to the Rev. R. G.
Livingstone, Rector of Brinkworth, for the loan of the
Laudian MS., to the Master and Fellows of Pembroke
College, Cambridge, for the loan of the MSS. in their
possession, and to several friends for help in various ways,
of which I hope they will accept this general acknow-
ledgement.

F. E. B.

Magdalen College,
    Nativity of S. John Baptist, 1903.

CONTENTS

CONTENTS

CONTENTS

INTRODUCTION

THE *Preces Privatae* of Lancelot Andrewes, the peculiar heritage
of the English Church from an age of astonishing fruitfulness
and distinction in devotional literature,[1] was compiled for his
own use and was not published till some years after his death.
It is a collection of material to supply the needs, daily and
occasional, of his own devotional life, providing for the great
departments of the life of the spirit—faith and hope and love,
praise and thanksgiving, penitence and petition. 'Of this
reverend prelate,' says John Buckeridge, his second successor
in the see of Ely, in his sermon at Andrewes' funeral,[2] 'I
may say *Vita eius vita orationis*, "his life was a life of
prayer"; a great part of five hours every day did he spend
in prayer to God. . . . And when his brother Master
Nicholas Andrewes died, he took that as a certain sign and
prognostic and warning of his own death, and from that time
till the hour of his own dissolution, he spent all his time in
prayer; and his prayer book, when he was in private, was
seldom seen out of his hands.' The *Preces Privatae* is a
monument of these hours of devotion, in which he first tested
for himself what he has bequeathed for us.

I

As sources of the text we still possess the three manuscripts
from which the printed editions have been derived, besides a
fourth of no independent value.

1. The most important of these is a copy given by the

---

[1] It is enough to notice here that the *Exercitia spiritualia* of S.
Ignatius Loyola (1491-1556) were published in 1548; the *Combatti-
mento spirituale* of Lorenzo Scupoli (1530-1610) in 1589; the *Vie
dévote* of S. François de Sales (1567-1622) in 1618; and the *Paradisus
animæ* of Jacob Merlo of Horst (1597-1644) in 1644.

[2] Andrewes *Sermons* v p. 296.

bishop himself to William Laud, which remained generally unknown until it was recovered from a dealer's stock and purchased in 1883 by Mr R. G. Livingstone, Fellow of Pembroke College, Oxford, and now Rector of Brinkworth in Gloucestershire. In form, it is a little paper book, $5 \times 2\frac{1}{2}$ in., of 188 pages with gilt edges, bound in white vellum and tied with four narrow green silk ribbands.[1] On the front cover is written in Laud's handwriting, 'My reverend Friend Bishop Andrews gave me this Booke a little before his death. W : Bath et Welles' ; and this is repeated below in a later hand, the original inscription having meanwhile faded. The text is unfinished, ending abruptly on p. 168, early in the course of the Evening Prayers, and the last 20 pages are left blank. The Greek is beautifully and, except for the accentuation, for the most part correctly written ; the Hebrew is scarcely beautiful and it is very incorrect. In the preface to his translation of the *Preces*, which will be referred to below, Richard Drake remarks, 'Had you seen the original manuscript, happy in the glorious deformity thereof, being slubbered with his pious hands and watered with his penitential tears, you would have been forced to confess, That book belonged to no other than pure and primitive devotion.'[2] It has been suggested[3] that the Laudian manuscript is the copy here referred to. But this is quite impossible : so far from being 'deformed' or 'slubbered' or 'watered,' the manuscript is quite clean and shows no signs of having been much used.[4] Neither is it probable that it is an autograph, as has been claimed for it.[5] Perhaps none of Andrewes' later Greek handwriting survives for comparison with the handwriting of the manuscript ; but in a copy of Demosthenes,[6] given to Andrewes by Dr Thomas Watts, who nominated him to his

[1] The book in the bishop's left hand in his portrait in the Hall of Jesus College, Oxford, is of the same form and may in fact be his prayer book.

[2] *A manual of the private devotions and meditations of . . . Lancelot Andrews . . . by* R. D., B.D., 1648, preface.

[3] By Mr Rackham in R. L. Ottley *Lancelot Andrewes*, append. D, p. 216.

[4] None of the passages from Andrewes which Laud incorporated in his own *Devotions* are contained in this MS. See below, p. lviii.

[5] By Mr Medd in his edition of the Laudian text, p. xii.

[6] Formerly belonging to R. W. Church, Dean of S. Paul's, and now to the Bishop of Oxford.

scholarship at Pembroke Hall, there are Greek marginal annotations, apparently in Andrewes' handwriting, and this writing is quite unlike that of the present manuscript. It may of course be said that the character of his handwriting as an undergraduate is no test of what it would be in his old age, and this MS. was written after his translation to Winchester in 1618. But on the other hand, his English hand remained steady: the signatures and Latin notes in the Demosthenes are apparently in the same hand as the papers of his mature life; while the Greek is of a different type from that of the manuscript of the *Preces* and such as would not naturally develop into it. Nor does the writing of the manuscript appear to shew any signs of old age. But what seems to be quite decisive is the Hebrew text: this is singularly incorrect and often unintelligible without emendation; and it is inconceivable that it can have been written by anyone who really understood Hebrew and could say his prayers in it; while the mistakes are just such as would be made by a copyist who knew little or nothing of the language beyond the alphabet, and did not understand what he was writing. It is almost certain therefore that the manuscript was written for the bishop by an amanuensis; and it may be conjectured that it was copied expressly for presentation to Laud, while its unfinished condition suggests that the copying was interrupted in order that the dying prelate might make the gift with his own hand.[1] The subsequent history of the manuscript, until its recovery by Mr Livingstone, is unknown. The only details that survive are the signature 'J. Mandevile' written in an 18th cent. hand on p. 188, and an entry from an auction catalogue of the 18th cent. pasted inside the back cover (p. 205), running as follows, 'Fifth Days S... | Friday, Januar... | Lot MANUSCR... | 592 The Psalms in Greek in the handwriting of Archbishop Andrews, and presented by him to Archbishop Laud, and 10 others,' the date being torn off; while in the upper left hand corner of the slip is written, 'Mowing's Auction Rooms, Maiden Lane, Covent Garden, W. Bristow Auctioneer.' This MS. is represented in the margin of the present volume by the symbol L.

[1] Laud does not notice any visit to Andrewes in his Diary of this date, and he records his death quite shortly, under Sept. 21, 1626.

2. After describing 'the original manuscript' as above, Drake adds that he had 'the happiness to obtain a copy under the fair hand of his [the bishop's] amanuensis.' This copy survives, and is preserved in the Library of Pembroke College, Cambridge, with an entry written and signed by Richard Drake himself to the effect that it was copied and given to him by his friend Samuel Wright, who had been secretary to Andrewes while bishop of Winchester, and was then Registrar to Matthew Wren bishop of Ely.[1] In form, the manuscript is a paper book, $6 \times 3\frac{3}{4}$ in., of 170 pages with gilt edges, bound in brown calf tooled in gold. The text is beautifully written, and although the writing is rather larger than that of the Laudian manuscript, it is possible, but by no means certain, that the two manuscripts are by the same hand. But there is considerable difference in their contents. The occasional variations in reading and some additions in Wright's copy are of little importance. The only considerable additions are the paragraph on p. 123 of the MS. (p. 197 below), and the whole of the concluding pages, 146-168, for which the last 20 blank pages of the Laudian MS. were evidently intended.[2] But the omissions are some of them more serious. They are of four kinds: (1) omissions of passages presumably not contained in the MS. from which Wright copied; viz. pp. 6, 7 (pp. 13-15 below), p. 18 ll. 16-19 (p. 40 ll. 18-21 below): (2) passages of purely personal application, of no direct practical use to anyone but the bishop himself, pp. 47, 119, 124 (pp. 61, 272, 223 below): (3) most of the Hebrew passages, very few of which, and those generally only single words and lines, are retained; while a few are rendered into Greek or the corresponding Septuagint text is substituted: (4) most of the petitions for the departed. In many or most cases under the last three heads, it is evident that the omissions are of what was contained in the text which Wright had before him, since their position is commonly marked by spaces in his copy. And perhaps in the case of the Hebrew, it was intended to insert at least some of it afterwards, and throughout for the most part the Hebrew that is retained

---

[1] *Amicissimus meus Samuel Wright Lanceloto Wintoniensi Epo olim à chartis, nunc autem Matthaeo Eliensi à Registris, pretiosum hoc κειμήλιον suâ manu accuratè descriptum dono dedit mihi Richardo Drake*

[2] Below pp. 108-112, 266, 121-124, 3, 4.

has the appearance of having been written in afterwards, perhaps by a different hand. In the matter of the petitions for the departed, those on pp. 55, 71, 86 of the Laudian MS. (pp. 59, 68, 78 below) are omitted simply without warning; the text runs straight on.[1] That on p. 13 below occurs in a passage two pages in length, which, as was noted above, was perhaps not contained in the exemplar from which Wright made his copy; while the positions of the petitions on pp. 85, 128 of the Laudian MS. (pp. 76, 101 below) are marked by blanks in Wright's copy (pp. 70, 111); and the petitions, for living and dead on p. 33, and for the unburied on p. 41, of L (pp. 48, 51), are retained by Wright (pp. 29, 35). The purpose of these omissions is not difficult to conjecture. It may be supposed that Wright's copy was prepared for an edition adapted to more or less popular use; and it might well be thought that the purely personal allusions would be only distracting, and the Hebrew unintelligible except to a very few; while the prayers for the departed might be regarded as unlikely to be welcome to the current opinion of the moment (1642-1648). For, although a proposed condemnation of prayers for the dead in a draft Article had been rejected in 1563, yet there was a strong feeling against them in some quarters in the 17th century, witness Donne's Sermon lxxii in 1626,[2] and Sir Thomas Browne's curious treatment of them as a 'heresy' in the early pages of the *Religio Medici* in 1642; while all that Andrewes has to say of them, outside the *Preces*, is 'For *offering* and *prayer for the dead*, there is little to be said against it; it cannot be denied that it is ancient.'[3]

But the MS. does not remain exactly in the condition in which it left Wright's hands: two sets of additions have been made to it. First, Drake has added throughout a large number of marginal references to the Scriptural sources, and from time to time corrected the text by the Septuagint; and on a flyleaf he has written Dean Nowell's distich *Officium vespertinum*, with Latin and English renderings of his

[1] The decisive words of that on p. 86 (78) are omitted in Mr Medd's text and translation.

[2] *Donne's Works* iii. pp 388 sqq. (ed. Alford).

[3] *Answer to Cardinal Perron* ix.

b

own.[1] And secondly, the whole MS. has been worked over by a second hand (apparently not Drake's) and corrected by a copy akin to the Laudian MS., but probably not identical with it in contents; with the result that several of Wright's omissions, including the personal references, have been supplied, and some new matter, not found in L, is added (p. 3*).[2] All these restorations and additions were made before 1675, when they appear in the *editio princeps* of the Greek text; and all of them, except the contents of pp. 6, 7,[3] are earlier than 1648, since they are represented in Drake's translation. This MS. is referred to below by the symbol W and the work of the second hand by W^2.

3. In the Barham Library, now belonging to the Master of Pembroke College, Cambridge, is a third MS., a paper book, $5\frac{7}{8} \times 3\frac{3}{4}$ in., of 144 pages with gold edges, the last 10 being left blank, except that on p. 142 is written Nowell's distich with Drake's renderings. The hand writing is poor and unequal. The text was evidently copied from Wright's MS. before it had been worked over by the second hand, *i.e.* at least before 1648; and it has obviously no independent value. This MS. is represented below by the symbol B.

4. The Harleian MS. 6614, in the British Museum, is a paper book, $6\frac{1}{8} \times 4$ in., of 154 pages with gilt edges, bound in stamped leather with two clasps. Only 84 of the pages are written on; the rest are blank. A note on the first page, originally signed with the initials of an unknown 'J. W.,' now almost obliterated by those of an equally unknown 'V. M.,' which are also stamped on the binding, says that the MS. is 'ex manu propria Lancelotti Andrews Wintoniensis olim episcopo, sicut a fide dignis accepi.' But the handwriting, a somewhat bold and irregular 17th cent. script, with obvious mistakes of reading, is certainly not that of Andrewes. The text is wholly Latin, and consists of devotions, certainly by Andrewes, but not corresponding to anything in the Greek. Their authenticity is sufficiently proved by their character as compared with the other works of Andrewes, and by the fact that a confession of faith, of which fragments are found in the 'second part' of the first and subsequent editions of the *Preces*, here occurs in full.

This MS. is referred to below by the symbol H.

---

[1] Below p. 104. [2] Below p. 9. [3] Below pp. 13-15.

II

The first form in which any part of the original text of the *Preces privatae* was given to the world, was that of an appendix to some copies of the *Verus Christianus* of Dr David Stokes, published at the Clarendon Press in 1668.[1] In this appendix the author gives a series of specimens, some in Greek, some in Latin, and one rendered into English, derived from the papers of Lancelot Andrewes, which he had 'received from several hands' (p. 56). Some of these have never hitherto appeared elsewhere; others, as will be seen immediately, form part of the current editions, in some cases in a text more developed and finished than that of Stokes' appendix, which evidently in these cases reproduces a preliminary draft of what was afterwards worked up more carefully. In fact these extracts throw some light on the genesis of the prayers and make it clear that the matter of them grew under the bishop's hand. Matter derived from this source is indicated below by the symbol S in the margin.

The first comprehensive edition of the *Preces*, the *textus receptus*, was edited by Dr John Lamphire, Principal of Hart Hall, and published at the Clarendon Press in 1675, with the *imprimatur*, dated March 16, 1673, of the Vice-Chancellor, Dr Ralph Bathurst, President of Trinity, and under the title *Rev. Patris Lanc. Andrews Episc. Winton. Preces Privatæ Græcè & Latinè*. The sources of this edition are threefold: first, Wright's MS. as we have it, that is, after Drake had made his corrections and additions, and after it had been worked over by the second hand, forming 'pars prima' of the whole; secondly, matter supplied to the editor by Richard Drake from Andrewes' papers, mostly in Latin, and here forming the 'pars secunda'; and thirdly, Stokes' appendix, from which are derived the Greek meditations on 'the Last Judgment' and 'the Shortness of Human Life' appended to the 'pars

[1] The Brit. Mus. copy has the appendix; that of the Bodleian has not.

prima,' and perhaps some of the paragraphs of the second part
which it has in common with Stokes. The Greek of the
first part is accompanied throughout by a parallel Latin
version printed on the opposite page. Two facts seem to
shew that, if this Latin as a whole is not to be attributed to
Andrewes, yet Lamphire at least used and incorporated the
Latin of Andrewes' papers, so far as it went. For first, in
a passage of which Stokes gives the Latin, Lamphire's
Latin is identical with Stokes', while it does not exactly
represent the parallel Greek ;[1] and secondly, while Lamphire shews no signs of any knowledge of Andrewes' Latin
sources, the Latin of his text agrees too closely with the
sources to be an independent rendering of the Greek.[2] By
way of appendix, Dr Lamphire has added, under a note,[3]
the Greek Morning and Evening Hymns, i.e. the *Gloria in
excelsis* and the Φῶς ἱλαρόν,[4] derived from Archbishop
Ussher's *de Romanæ ecclesiæ Symbolo apostolico vetere*, published in 1647; and a Greek Ode on the Passion, written
Ap. 19, 1633, by Thomas Master, Fellow of New College,
apparently taken, along with the accompanying Latin version
by Henry Jacob of Merton, from a pamphlet published at
Oxford in 1658, under the title *D. Henrici Savilii τοῦ
μακαρίτου, Oratio, coram regina Elizabetha Oxoniæ habita ;
aliæque doctiss. virorum opellæ posthumæ*.[5] This edition is
referred to as O.

This text of the *Preces* was republished in two sizes in

---

[1] Lamphire p. 73=Stokes p. 22=pp. 59 sq., 269 below.

[2] See pp. 59 sq. (p. 52 ll. 20-30 below), 93 (69 ll. 27-37), 173 (277).

[3] P. 351 : *Sequitur Hymnus Matutinus usûs antiquissimi in Ecclesiâ, ex MS*. Alexandrino *Bibliothecæ Regiæ. Accedit & Vespertinus, quia vetus. De utroque consulendus est Rev*. Usserius, *p*. 41, 43. *l*. de Symbolis. The text of the *Gloria in excelsis* is not in fact that of Cod. Alex.; see note on p. 23 l. 11 below.

[4] Below pp. 23, 104.

[5] This pamphlet contained also an English verse translation of the Ode by Abraham Cowley. T. Master, who was a friend of Lamphire's, had a considerable reputation as a writer of Greek odes. See *Dict. National Biog.* vol. xxxvii under his name. The Ode was published separately with an English translation in Εἰς τὴν τοῦ Χριστοῦ σταύρωσιν μονοστροφικά : *an ode on the Crucifixion of Christ : being a paraphrase of a Greek Hymn at the end of Bishop Andrewes' Devo-tions*, by R-t T-r, A.M. Greek and English. Edinb. 1742.

1828, with a new Latin preface, and some corrections and added references, by Peter Hall, under the title *Reverendi Patris Lanceloti Andrews episc : Wintoniensis Preces Privatæ Quotidianæ Græce et Latine : editio altera et emendatior* (London, Pickering) ; and an *editio tertia et emendatior* was issued by an anonymous editor and the same publisher in 1848, being Peter Hall's edition, with a short additional preface explaining that some rearrangements of the text of 1675 have been made and the references corrected. It was again independently edited in 1853 for the Library of Anglo-Catholic Theology, by Dr John Barrow, Principal of S. Edmund Hall, who collated Lamphire's text with Wright's copy and Stokes' appendix, and added as 'pars tertia' the Latin devotions of the Harleian MS., which were here printed for the first time. In 1865 Mr Frederick Meyrick, now Prebendary of Lincoln and Rector of Blickling, began a new edition with a beautifully printed issue of the Latin of the first part ; in 1867 he added the Greek, in 1870 the second part, and in 1873 the third part. Again, in 1895, Mr Henry Veale, sometime Rector of Newcastle-under-Lyme, re-edited the first and second parts, with added headlines, marginal numberings, introduction, notes, etc., of no value.

Meanwhile, in 1892 Mr P. G. Medd, Rector of North Cerney, edited for the S.P.C.K. the text of the then recently recovered Laudian MS., supplying the blank at the end from Wright's copy, correcting the Hebrew, adding an apparatus of the readings of the Cambridge MSS. and the *textus receptus,* and in an introduction giving a history of the text. Unfortunately the reproduction of the text of L leaves something to be desired in point of accuracy.

III

So far we have been concerned with the MSS. and printed editions of the Greek and Latin of the *Preces.* But the book was given to the world in an English translation some time before any part of the original text was published.

In 1630 appeared *Institutiones piæ or directions to pray* by H. I. (London, Henry Seile). 'H. I.' is Henry Isaacson of Pembroke Hall, Cambridge, who lived with Andrewes for some time as his secretary. In the fourth edition of this work, published in 1655, after the date of Isaacson's death early in the same year, the title is altered to *Holy devotions with directions to pray . . . by the Right Reverend Father in God Lancelot Andrewes, late Bishop of Winchester ;* and in a new preface by Henry Seile the publisher, it is said : 'the true father and primary author of these Devotions was the glory of this Church, the great and eminent Andrews . . . and thus the parentage of this Book, which, like that of Cyrus, was, for divers years, concealed under a Shepherd's cottage, (a good and faithful Shepherd he was that concealed it) comes now to be vindicated to its own nativity : and the Child being of full age, desires to be known abroad in the world for her Father's daughter, the daughter of her true, not supposed Father.' In this form the book was re-issued several times up to 1684, and in 1834 it was rearranged and edited anew by W. H. Hale, Preacher of the Charter-house. The new title and the statements of the preface are so far true to the facts, that the book certainly contains passages of considerable length which are found elsewhere among Andrewes' devotions ; and other passages, which cannot be so verified, would seem from their method and character to be worked up from material supplied by him ; and his influence is clear throughout. But the book as a whole cannot be ascribed to Andrewes. The form and style of the bulk of it is not in his manner. It has not seemed desirable to include in the present edition any of its contents, except what it has in common with other sources.[1]

In 1647 Humphrey Moseley published the *Private Devotions by the Right Reverend Father in God Lancelot Andrewes, late Bishop of Winchester,* a 12mo volume consisting of fragments of the matter which later editions have made familiar and a few things from the sermons, with very little, and that of no importance, which does not occur elsewhere. In range and general character it is quite unlike

---

[1] The *Institutiones piæ* is the source of what is attributed to Andrewes in Spinckes *The true Church of England Man's Companion to the Closet, or a complete Manual of Private Devotions* 1749 (frequently reprinted), and of the Litany in *A Litany and Prayers of the Holy Communion by Bp. Andrewes* London, Jas. Burns, 1844.

what has generally been known as 'Bp. Andrewes' Devotions.'
On its publication, Richard Drake, who had been a scholar
of Andrewes' College, 'finding' in it, as he says, 'a great
invasion made upon' the bishop's 'honour,' 'resolved to
pay' his 'due respects to his precious memory and to
exercise so much charity, which' he 'had learned from his
devotions, towards others, and not to engross to' his 'own
private use and benefit, what' he 'was confident would be
most serviceable and welcome to the Church of God,' but
to publish an adequate version of the *Preces* from the copy
he had obtained from Dr Wright. Accordingly the same
publisher issued *A manual of the private devotions and meditations of the Right Reverend Father in God Lancelot Andrews,
late Lord Bishop of Winchester : translated out of a fair Greek
MS. of his Amanuensis by* R. D., *B.D.*, the preface being
dated S. John Baptist's Day, 1648. This version represents
Wright's MS. after most of the additions had been made by
the second hand.[1] It was re-issued in *A manual of Private
Devotions with a manual of directions for the Sick, by Lancelot
Andrews, late Bishop of Winchester,* London, 1670; and
subsequent editions appeared in 1674, 1682, 1692. In
1853 it was re-edited 'with corrections' in the *Churchman's
Library*, and in 1854 by James Bliss in the *Library of
Anglo-Catholic Theology*,[2] and a selection from it, with
corrections, was published in 1855 and onwards in *A
Manual of Private Devotions* (London, Masters).

Another translation, if so it can be called, made from the
editio princeps of 1675, was published in 1730, under the title
*Private Prayers translated from the Greek Devotions of Bp.
Andrewes, with additions by Geo. Stanhope D.D.* Dr
Stanhope, Dean of Canterbury, died in 1728, and this
edition was published from his papers with a preface by J.
Hutton, of King's College, Cambridge. It was re-edited
by George Horne, Dean of Canterbury and President of
Magdalen College, Oxford, afterwards Bishop of Norwich,
between 1781 and 1790, and re-issued by the S.P.C.K.
from 1808 onwards. Dr Stanhope's rendering can scarcely
be called a translation : it is rather a grandiloquent paraphrase,
with omissions and insertions and alterations which effectively
obliterate the point and conciseness of the original. Its

[1] See above, p. xviii. [2] Andrewes *Minor Works*, pp. 223 sqq.

contents are chiefly the (Greek) morning and evening prayers, the morning prayers for a week, and the Dial. It was abridged and supplied with references by Burton Bouchier in *Prayers and offices of private devotion* (London, 1834); and reprinted as a whole, with part of Hutton's preface, an introduction, references, irrelevant notes, etc., and a supplement of prayers altered from some of those of the Book of Common Prayer, by Jos. Macardy in *The Heart: its meditations and exercises, comprising private prayers from the Greek devotions of Lancelot Andrews by George Stanhope, late Dean of Canterbury. Also from approved authorities an introduction, notes and supplement* (London, 1843). It was also the source of what is derived from Andrewes in *A few forms of morning and evening prayer, adapted for private and family devotion, from the works of Bishop Andrewes*, etc., by Stuart Corbett (London, 1827).

A new version was made by Peter Hall and published by Pickering in 1830, under the title *The Private Devotions of Lancelot Andrews, Bishop of Winchester, translated from the Greek and Latin . . . to which is added the Manual for the Sick by the same learned prelate: second edition corrected,* and it was re-issued in 1839, with additions to the preface.

In 1839 also, Edward Bickersteth, Rector of Walton, published a new translation of both the first and the second parts, with added titles and some emendations, in his work *The Book of Private Devotions, containing a collection of the most valuable early devotions of the Early Reformers and their successors in the Church of England.*

The 78th of the *Tracts for the Times*, published in 1840, consisted of *The Greek Devotions of Bishop Andrewes translated and arranged* by John Henry Newman, in a version of which R. W. Church has said that it is ' one of those rare translations which make an old book new.'[1] It embraces nearly the whole of the First Part, with some rearrangements, the object of which is not always clear. The version was re-issued with a preface and in a more tractable form in 1842 (Oxford, Parker). In 1844 John Mason Neale, in *Private Devotions of Bishop Andrewes translated from the Latin* (Oxford, Parker), completed the work with a version of the Second Part, omitting some fragmentary or perplexing

[1] *Pascal and other Sermons,* Lond. 1896, p. 86.

passages.   This translation sometimes misses the sense : but
it is not unworthy to stand beside Card. Newman's version of
the Greek.   The two were afterwards combined ; and it is
in this form that the Devotions have since been most easily
accessible.   These translations supplied the prayers for communion in *A Litany and Prayers of the Holy Communion*
(London, Jas. Burns, 1844), and were the source of J. W.
H. M[olyneux'] *Private prayers for members of the Church
of England selected from the devotions of Bishop Andrewes*
(London 1866, 1883), and formed the basis of *The Mantle
of Prayer : a book of devotions compiled chiefly from those of
Bishop Andrewes* (London, Masters, 1881) by A. N. with
a preface by W. J. Butler, afterwards Dean of Lincoln.

In 1883 the late Edmund Venables, Precentor of Lincoln,
revised these translations, chiefly in the way of substituting
the language of the Authorised Version and the Prayer Book
in quotations which Newman and Neale had re-rendered, and
supplying Neale's omissions, and re-edited the whole, with a
preface by J. R. Woodford, Bishop of Ely, and an interesting introduction of his own (*The Private Devotions of
Lancelot Andrewes*, new ed., London, Suttaby, 1883).   In
1896 Dr Alexander Whyte of S. George's Free Church,
Edinburgh, in *Lancelot Andrewes and his Private Devotions :
a biography, a transcript and an interpretation* (Edinburgh)
rearranged a large part of the devotions, mainly following
Newman and Neale's versions, and prefixed to them a
depreciation of Andrewes and an interesting, but perhaps
extravagant, appreciation of the devotions.   And lastly,
these versions are the basis of Mr J. E. Kempe's *Private
Devotions of Bishop Andrewes selected and arranged with
variations adapted to general use* (London S.P.C.K., 1897),
in which the very large ' variations ' were made ' with some
reference to hints by Stanhope.'

Finally, in 1899 Mr Medd published an English translation of the Laudian MS. uniform with his edition of the
text.

IV

The life of Lancelot Andrewes has often been written,
and it is not proposed to rewrite it here.   It is sufficient for

the present purpose to recall the outlines of his history and the chief aspects of his character.

He was the son of John Andrewes, Master of Trinity House, and was born in 1555 in Thames St. in the parish of All Hallows Barking and baptized in the parish church by the Tower. He was sent first to the Cooper's Free School of Ratcliffe, in the parish of Stepney, under Master Ward, and then to the recently founded Merchant Taylors' under the headmastership of Richard Mulcaster. In 1571 he went up to Cambridge as a scholar of Pembroke Hall on the foundation of Dr Thomas Watts, Archdeacon of Middlesex, who nominated him to one of his six scholarships; and in the same year he was nominated by the Queen to a scholarship at Jesus College, Oxford, by the advice of the founder of the College. He took his degree in 1575, and was elected a fellow of Pembroke Hall in 1576; after which he resided till 1586, visiting his home for a month at Easter in each year; and during his holiday in 1580 he witnessed the earthquake which destroyed part of S. Paul's and, as we shall see, made a lasting impression on his mind. He was ordained deacon in 1580 and priest some time between this and 1585,[1] when he took his B.D. As Catechist of his College he lectured on the Decalogue, and the substance of his lectures is preserved in *The Pattern of Catechistical Doctrine*. In 1586 Henry Earl of Huntingdon, President of the North, made him his chaplain and took him with him to York, where, it is noticed, he reconciled many Roman Catholics to the English Church. Soon after, he became chaplain to Whitgift, Archbishop of Canterbury, and to the Queen. In 1589 Walsingham procured his presentation to the cure of S. Giles' Cripplegate, and to a prebend at Southwell, and later in the same year to the stall of S. Pancras in S. Paul's. Of his work at S. Giles' and S. Paul's, the S. Giles' sermons and the S. Paul's lectures on Genesis remain as monuments in the *Apospasmatia*.[2] In the same year, 1589, he was elected Master of his College in

---

[1] Sixteen years before his *Judgment of the Lambeth Articles* (*Cat. doct.* p. 294); so probably in 1580 or 1581.

[2] ΑΠΟΣΠΑΣΜΑΤΙΑ SACRA *or a collection of posthumous and orphan lectures delivered at St Pauls and St Giles his Church* . . . *never before extant* London, 1657.

succession to Fulke, and held the office till 1605. In 1597 he became a prebendary of Westminster, and in 1601 succeeded Goodman as Dean ; and in this capacity he assisted, in the office belonging to the Dean of Westminster, at the Coronation of James I on S. James' Day 1603, the first coronation celebrated in English. In 1604 he took part in the Hampton Court Conference, where he was especially prominent in the defence of the sign of the cross in baptism ; [1] and in the same year he was appointed one of the translators of what became the 'Authorised Version' of the Bible, published in 1611. In 1605 he was consecrated to the see of Chichester, in succession to Antony Watson, became Lord High Almoner, and resigned the Mastership of Pembroke Hall. While bishop of Chichester he began his controversy with 'Matthaeus Tortus,' Cardinal Robert Bellarmin, and published *Tortura Torti* in 1609, in which year he was translated to Ely, in succession to Martin Heaton, and here he continued the controversy by the publication of the *Responsio ad Apologiam Cardinalis Bellarmini* in 1610. On the death of Bancroft in this year, it was generally expected that Andrewes would succeed to the see of Canterbury ; but this was not to be, and Abbot became archbishop. In 1618 Andrewes was translated to Winchester, as successor to James Montague, and in 1619 became Dean of the Chapel Royal. In 1621 he was one of the group of peers who attended Francis Bacon to accept the acknowledgment of his confession made to the Upper House; and in the same year, as a member of the commission in Abbot's irregularity, incurred by accidental homicide, he checked the severe judgment of his colleagues and secured an opinion favourable to the metropolitan. In the beginning of 1625 he was unable, through his own illness, to attend the King in his last sickness, and on Sept. 26 of the next year himself died, and was buried on Nov. 11 behind the high altar of S. Saviour's, Southwark, where his tomb and effigy are still to be seen.

In his preface to the *Holy devotions with directions to pray*— that is, the second edition of the *Institutiones piæ*—Henry Seile sums up the life of Andrewes in the words, 'Dr Andrews in the School, Bishop Andrews in the Pulpit,

[1] Cardwell *Conferences* p. 198.

Saint Andrews in the Closet.' And this represents the three conspicuous aspects of the life of the prelate, as scholar and theologian, ecclesiastic, and saint.

1. He was pre-eminently a scholar. His studiousness began in his early years, and was excessive. As a schoolboy he had to be forced to play games, and as an undergraduate he disliked both indoor and outdoor games and found his recreation in walking, whether with a companion with whom he discussed what interested him, or alone, occupying himself with the observation of nature, which continued to be his chief relaxation all his life long, and supplied the basis of a knowledge of natural science which was not merely dilettante but was recognised as something more by Francis Bacon, who notes that he had pretensions to some experiments.[1] At school he made brilliant progress in Latin, Greek, and Hebrew; and at Cambridge he was among the first representatives of the reviving Greek scholarship. His Easter holiday in London was generally devoted to getting some knowledge of a new language, with the result that he became a considerable linguist, till, in Fuller's whimsical words, he was 'so skilled in all (especially oriental) languages, that some conceived he might, if then living, have served as interpreter-general in the confusion of tongues.'[2] He was among the most considerable, if not himself the most considerable, of English scholars, in an age of great scholars, with something of an European reputation; the correspondent of Cluverius and Vossius, of Grotius, Erpenius and Heinsius, the closest friend of Casaubon, the literary censor of Bacon—his 'inquisitor,' as Bacon calls him—the associate of Selden, the friend and encourager of his brilliant juniors, George Herbert[3] and John Donne,[4] and the thoughtful and munificent patron of plenty of young and promising scholars, and, as Dean of Westminster, the keen promoter of the interests of Westminster School. After taking his master's degree, he devoted himself chiefly to Theology, and his lectures as Catechist of Pembroke Hall attracted large audiences from the whole University and the surrounding country. He was a man

---

[1] Bacon *Works*, ed. Ellis and Spedding, iv p. 63.
[2] Fuller *Church History of Britain* xi 17 §46.
[3] I. Walton *Life of Mr George Herbert*.
[4] Jessop *John Donne* p. 51.

after the Second Solomon's own heart, and the King turned
to him to defend him against the assaults of the great
Bellarmin, who attacked the imposition of the oath on
Roman Catholics after the Gunpowder Plot; with the result
that against his will and inclination he became the official
controversialist of the English Church, and proved its
adequate defender when the guns of the new Jesuit learning
were turned upon it. He also replied to Cardinal Perron's
strictures on the Anglican position, and carried on a controversy with the protestant du Moulin. His library, so far as
can be judged from that part of it which he bequeathed to
Pembroke Hall, while chiefly theological, was yet of considerable range.[1] And his learning is conspicuous enough in
his works, where, learned as they obviously are, and found to
be still more so if anyone will be at the pains to examine
their sources, he does not think it necessary, after the modern
fashion, to give references for all he has to say. His extra-
ordinarily minute knowledge of the Holy Scriptures is plain
to everybody; and his command of it and of the rest of his
learning, is such that it perhaps serves to conceal his originality. His wealth of reminiscence is such, and is so inwrought
into the texture of his mind, that he instinctively uses it to
express anything he has to say. To one to whom knowledge
is so large an element in life and is itself so living a thing;
whose learning is so assimilated as to be identified with his
spontaneous self, and has become as available as language
itself, originality and reminiscence become in a measure identical; the new can be expressed as a combination of older
elements. But originality was scarcely the chief note of his
mind. He is marked rather by great, solid and readily-
available learning than by great original ideas. He was
scholarly, historical, inductive, rather than speculative and
creative. His imagination was collective and organising, as
it were, rather than originative. It showed itself in new
combinations of existing material, rather than in substantively
new contributions. He took up what he found and fused it
into a new whole, and that often with something of real
poetic distinction. He was a scholar, with a scholar's in-
stinct for analysis and sense of the value of words and appreciation of form. But he was not a *litterateur*. His English

[1] See the list in *Minor Works* p. cxiv. sqq.

style has been criticised, and justly. In formal composition he was not happy, so far as we have the means of judging. And in the period of his mature life, we have not much to judge from; for the great sermons are scarcely formal compositions, for all the pains he bestowed on them; they are rather exhaustive notes, written under the stimulus of a vivid imagination of a congenial audience, and in language not strictly literary but colloquial and in a way casual, and obviously different from what he used when he was writing to be read and not to be heard. It is clear, from what was said of him as a preacher, that his delivery was a very real part of the charm of his sermons; and perhaps no one could read them aloud with effect who did not possess a considerable faculty of dramatic interpretation. This applies chiefly to the great sermons which belong mostly to his later life. With the earlier ones the case is rather different; it seems clear that they are much more of the nature of formal compositions, and were not written under the same conditions. His audiences at S. Giles' and S. Paul's were not so congenial intellectually as the more educated audiences of the Court, and this probably reacted on his style; he had to compose his sermons, rather than to make notes, with the consequence that in form they were rather dull and unadorned. Besides, he was less experienced, and perhaps had not yet gained the colloquial confidence of his later years. But perhaps there is a reason for the defect of his English style quite apart from this. Isaac Williams has accounted for his own defective style by the fact that as a boy he habitually thought in Latin, and his written English was a translation of Latin thoughts.[1] It is probable that the same was the case more or less with Andrewes, and that Latin was his language of soliloquy; and he lived too habitually in the medium of other languages than his mother-tongue to leave his English style much chance. His sermons are full of Latin and Greek, and he gives precedence to the Vulgate in reciting his text. It was the habit of preachers of his day to interlard their sermons with Latin; and sometimes this degenerates into a mere trick with a result as ludicrous as that of Buckeridge's sermon at Andrewes' funeral, in which the Latin seems often to be nothing but a quite gratuitous trans-

[1] *Autobiography* pp. 5, 21.

lation of what is just going to be said in English. But this
is not so with Andrewes; his Latin and Greek and Hebrew
has a reason, whether as the *ipsissima verba* of what he is
quoting, or as adding something to the point and clearness
and exactness of what he is saying. His Latin composition,
in the *Opuscula* and the controversy with Bellarmin, is perhaps
livelier and readier than his formal English; but it is not the
living, lucid, limpid tongue of the Middle Ages, but the ar-
tificial classicised Latin that resulted from the Renaissance. Of
his Greek perhaps no specimen remains outside the Devotions.

2. As an ecclesiastic Andrewes was the most notable
man of his day in England. He was rising under Elizabeth
and might earlier have taken the lead if he had been willing
to accept the bishoprics that were offered him at the price of
the sacrilege which he loathed, the sacrifice of their revenues
to the Tudor rapacity. Under James I he soon found his
level. His experience was varied and representative. As
Catechist of his College, as Chaplain to the President of the
North and to Whitgift, as Vicar of S. Giles' and canon of
Southwell, S. Paul's, and Westminster, and Dean of the last,
and as bishop successively of Chichester, Ely and Winchester,
he had experience of most of the possible spheres and conditions of ecclesiastical life. And in them all he represented
a new type which was emerging after the degradation of the
preceding period. What the general standard was and what
he thought of it, can be gathered from his Convocation
sermon in 1593,[1] where he holds up the mirror to the clergy,
and especially to the bishops, and lashes their unworthiness—
their sloth and neglect and indifference, their want of learning
and the ineptitude of their preaching, their servility to the
great, their low standard of life, their laborious solicitude for
their own interests and neglect of those of their flocks and of
the good of the Church, their indifference as well about error
in doctrine and life as about the edification of the faithful,
their spoliation of the Church and venal dispensations and
general rapacity, their scandalous ordinations, their simony
and sacrilege and the prostitution of ecclesiastical censures.
This, and more, is what men think of them, and he tells them
that it is true, and warns them that men's eyes are on them,
and that if they will not attend to their flocks, their flocks will

[1] *Opuscula posthuma* pp. 29 sqq.

soon attend to them. It is interesting to compare this sermon
with Colet's famous Convocation sermon eighty years before.
After sixty years of professed reformation, the state of things is
very much what it was; only Andrewes' picture is darker and
his chastisement more severe. From this, and from the in-
quiries in his Visitation Articles something can be gathered of
what he thought the standard of clerical life ought to be and
of what he aimed at in his own life. There is not much
recorded of the details of his ecclesiastical life. To the
generality he would chiefly be known as a preacher and as
the great preacher of his day. He was a 'painful' preacher,
taking infinite trouble with his sermons; he said of himself
that if he preached twice in a day, he prated once. Of his
sermons, besides the famous 96, there survive the 19 on
Prayer and the Lord's Prayer, the 7 on the *Temptation*, a
number of parochial sermons at S. Giles', and the lectures on
the early chapters of Genesis given partly at S. Paul's,
partly at S. Giles'. Their learning and compact matter
indicate the perhaps over-severe standard he applied when
he complained of the ignorant ineptitude of contemporary
preaching. But as the most notable preacher of his day, he
used his opportunity to rebuke and counteract the 'auricular
profession,' as he calls it, of an age which exaggerated the
importance of preaching, and to insist that the hearing of
sermons is not the chief part of religious observance, and that
the Word is the stimulus to devotion and is useless unless it
issue in this and in its central highest act, the communion of
the Eucharist. Perhaps the only detail of his spiritual minis-
tration which is explicitly recorded is that as Prebendary of
S. Pancras, and therefore *ex officio* Penitentiary, he attended
in the north aisle of S. Paul's in Lent in readiness for any
who desired to consult him. It is needless to say that this
resulted in a charge of 'popery.' In his sermon on *Absolution*
he expounds the doctrine and bearing of the power of the
keys. For the exercise of the 'key of knowledge' he had
qualified himself while at Cambridge and had become 'well-
seen in cases of conscience' and acquired a reputation as a
casuist. His sense of the neglect of this key he expresses in
another sermon. 'I take it to be an error .. to think the fruits
of repentance, and the worth of them, to be a matter any
common man can skill of well enough; needs never ask

St John or St Paul what he should do; knows what he should do as well as St Paul or St John either. And that it is not rather a matter wherein we need the counsel and direction of such as are professed that way. Truly it is neither the least, nor the last, part of our learning to be able to give answer and direction in this point. But therefore laid aside and neglected by us, because not sought after by you. Therefore not studied, but by very few, *quia nemo nos interrogat*, because it is grown out of request quite. We have learned, I know not where, a new, a shorter course, which flesh and blood better likes of. To pass the whole course of our life, and, in the whole course of our life, not to be able to set down, where, or when, or what we did, when we did that which we call repenting; what fruits there came of it; what those fruits might be worth. And but even a little before our death (and as little as may be), not till the world have given us over, then, lo, to come to our *quid faciemus?* to ask, "what we should do?" when we are able to do nothing. And then must one come, and (as we call it) speak comfortably to us, that is, minister to us a little Divinity laudanum, rather stupefactive for the present than doing any sound good; and so take our leaves to go meet with *ira ventura*. This way, this fashion of repenting, St John knew it not; it is far from his *fructus dignos;* St Paul knew it not; it is far from his *opera digna*. And I can say little to it, but I pray God it deceive us not.'[1] In the 16th of his Visitation articles is an inquiry as to the violation of the seal of confession.

In the sermons again Andrewes complains of the want of worship and its expression in his day. 'Now, adoration is laid aside, and with the most, neglected quite. Most come and go without it, nay they scarce know what it is. And with how little reverence, how evil beseeming us, we use ourselves in the church, coming in thither, staying there, departing thence, let the world judge. Why? What are we to the glorious saints in heaven? Do not they worship thus? Off go their "crowns," down "before the throne they cast them," and "fall down" themselves after, when they worship. Are we better than they? Nay, are we better than his saints on earth, that have ever seemed to go toc far, rather than to come too short in this

[1] *Sermon Repent. and Fasting* viii (i pp. 450 sq.).

c

point.'[1] 'Our religion and *cultus* must be uncovered, and a bare-faced religion; we would not use to come before a mean prince, as we do before the King of kings and Lord of lords, even the God of heaven and earth. "The four and twenty elders fell down before Him that sat on the throne, and worshipped Him that liveth for ever, and cast their crowns before His throne." The wandering eye must learn to be "fastened on Him" and "the work of justice" and "peace." The worship of the "knees" "to bow" and "kneel before the Lord their maker." Our feet are to "come before his face; for the Lord is a great God and a great King above all gods." Jacob though he were not able to stand or kneel, yet because he would use some corporal service "leaned upon his staff and worshipped God." . . . This must be done as duty due unto God.'[2] Accordingly, Andrewes was the 'ritualist' of his day. In Prynne's indictment of Archbishop Laud, there is produced a plan of Andrewes' chapel, and a description of his altar with its lights and cushions, the canister for the wafers and the basin for the oblations, the cruet for the 'water of mixture,' the credence and provision for the lavatory, the censer and incense-boat, copes and altar-cloths and veil.[3] And in the *Notes on the Book of Common Prayer*[4] there is an elaborate ceremonial of the altar, which if carried out to-day, would perhaps even now be surprising. Henry Isaacson, Andrewes' chaplain and biographer, remarks on the impression produced by the worship of the chapel at Ely: 'the souls of many that *obiter* came thither in time of divine service, were very much elevated, and they stirred up to the like reverend deportment. Yea some that had been there were so taken with it, that they desired to end their days in the bishop of Ely's chapel.'[5] But he did not enforce his own standard of worship on other people; he was 'content with the enjoying without the enjoining.'[6]

---

[1] *Serm. Gunpowder Treason* ix (iv p. 374).

[2] *Serm. Temptation* (v p. 554): cf. *ib.* pp. 60, 231, i p. 262, *Opuscula posthuma* p. 49.

[3] See *Minor Works* pp. xcvii sqq.

[4] *Minor Works* pp. 151 sqq. Notice his frank assertion of the pagan analogues and origins of Christian ceremonies in *A discourse of ceremonies* (*Cat. doct.* p. 365 sqq.).

[5] *Minor Works* p. xiii.

[6] Fuller *Church History* xi 48.

3. The saintly character of the 'good bishop' was recognised by his contemporaries. His 'whiteness of soul' inspired reverence; and in the court of James I he alone could awe the royal chatterbox into some silence.[1] Those who knew him dwell upon his zeal and piety, as illustrated by his hours of private devotion, the worship of his chapel, and his strict observance of Lent and Embertides and the other fasts; his charity and munificence, as exemplified by his large and ever-increasing and thoughtful alms during his lifetime, and his imaginative bequests, which were characteristically minute in their application, on his death; his fidelity in the discharge of his public duties, in the maintenance and improvement of the property entrusted to him in his several benefices, in the distribution of his patronage, and his hatred of simony and sacrilege and usury, and in the exercise of the influence which his position gave him for the promotion of the right men; his gratitude to his benefactors, in his care for them, their memory and their families; his generous hospitality, especially to scholars and strangers; his affability and geniality, his 'extraordinary kindness' and 'wonderful memory' for persons and places, and his 'grave facetiousness'; and his modesty and humility.[2]

And all this was grounded in a large, clear and definite theology. 'From *nescitis* cometh no good; without knowledge the soul itself is not good. *Nescitis quid petatis*—no good prayer; *adoratis quod nescitis*—no good worship. And so, ignorant devotion, implicit faith, blind obedience all rebuked. Zeal, if not *secundum scientiam*, can not be *secundum conscientiam*.'[3] His theology is the Catholic Faith, neither pared away on the one hand, nor embellished with questionable deductions on the other. '*Compass Sion and go round about her.* For one Canon given of God, two testaments, three symbols, the four first councils, five centuries and the series of Fathers therein, fix the rule of religion.'[4] So stated this might no doubt easily be criticised; but in substance it represents the defensible position arrived at consciously or unconsciously by the English Church. It repre-

[1] *Ib.* 46.
[2] See *Minor Works* pp. xii-xxv.
[3] *Serm. Gunpowder Tr.* iii (iv p. 250).
[4] *Opuscula* p. 90; *Respons. ad Bellarm.* p. 26.

sents to Andrewes the proportionate Catholic religion—what
he fought for in the confusions of his time, distinguishing it
on the one hand from vain speculations and intrusions into
what we do not and can not know, from vain imaginations
and 'idiolatries' positive and negative, and on the other from
dubious deductions claiming to be of faith.   There are for
him such things as *principal* doctrines, and 'there is no *principal dogma* in which we do not agree with the Fathers and
they with us.'[1]   Everything is not on the same level and
equally essential.   And so—' Blessed be God that among
divers other mysteries about which there are so many mists
and clouds of controversies raised in all ages and even in this
of ours, hath yet left us some clear and without controversy ;
manifest and yet great ; and again great and yet manifest.
So great as no exception to be taken ; so manifest as no
question to be made about them.   Withal, to reform our
judgments in this point.   For a false conceit is crept into the
minds of men, to think the points of religion that be manifest
to be certain petty points scarce worth the hearing.   Those
—yea those be great and none but those, that have great
disputes about them.   It is not so : $\tau\grave{\alpha}$ $\mu\grave{\epsilon}\nu$ $\mathring{\alpha}\nu\alpha\gamma\kappa\alpha\hat{\iota}\alpha$ &c.
Those that are necessary He hath made plain : those that
are not plain, not necessary.   What better proof than this
here ?   [1 Tim. iii 16.]   This here a mystery, a great one
—religion hath no greater—yet manifest and *in confuso* with
all Christians.   Zachary's prophecy and promise touching
Christ, wherewith he concludeth his *Benedictus* (we hear it
every day) shall not deceive us for this mystery : He came
" to guide our feet into the way of peace."   A way of peace
then there shall be whereof all parts shall agree, even in the
midst of a world of controversies.   That there need not such
ado in complaining, if men did not delight rather to be tread-
ing mazes than to walk in the ways of peace.   For even still
such a way there is, which lieth fair enough and would lead
us sure enough to salvation, if leaving those other rough
labyrinths we would but be " shod with the preparation of
the Gospel of peace."   Yea further the Apostle doth assure
us that if whereunto we are come and wherein we all agree,
we would constantly proceed by the rule, these things wherein
we are " otherwise minded," even them would God reveal

---

[1] *Respons. ad Bellarm.* p. 70.

unto us. That is he maketh no controversy but controversies would cease, if conscience were made of the practice of that which is out of controversy. And I would to God it were so, and that this here and such other *manifeste magna* were in account. With the Apostle himself it was so . . . in that having been "ravished in spirit up to the third heavens and there heard wonderful high mysteries past man's utterance"; yet reckoned he all those nothing in comparison of this plain mystery here, nay "esteemed himself not to know anything at all" but this.'[1] In broad outline the theology which he preached, and in which he apparently hoped that the practice of that which is out of controversy would generally issue, is the Creed, professed by a Catholic Church, wherein the Holy Ghost, through a ministry of apostolic succession and divine right,[2] regenerates men in baptism, confirms them by the imposition of hands, absolves them by a second imposition of hands, in the exercise of the keys, 'the Church's act,' by which 'God ordinarily proceedeth'[3]; feeds them with the body and blood of Christ our Lord in the most holy mysteries of the Eucharist, which impart what they represent, in which there is at once a sacrifice and a communion.[4] In the Church, men, 'not trusting in their own righteousness,'[5] are to live in faith and hope and love, in a disciplined life of penitence and its fruits and obedience to the commandments, in prayer and fasting and almsgiving, bringing forth the fruit of the Spirit in order, peace and comeliness. With this as the clue he was free to range over the broad field of Holy Scripture and literature and experience, and to illustrate and expand and embellish it with all that knowledge and imagination could find there. In this he looked for that peace, of which he was 'avidior fortasse quam par est.'[6] In an age when men were for penetrating the mysteries of the divine predestination and making it the substance of religion, Andrewes strove to call them back to the 'plain mystery' of the Faith, and avowed that in the 16 years since he was

---

[1] *Serm. Nativity* iii (i p. 35); cf. *ib.* xi (i p. 191).
[2] *Opuscula posthuma*, pp. 183, 187; *Serm. Absolution* (v 92).
[3] *Serm. Pent.* v (iii 191), *Absolution* (v 93).
[4] *Serm. Res.* xii (ii 402), *Nativ.* xii (i 213); *Res.* vii (ii 300), *Imagin.* (v 66 sq.); and conclusions of Christmas, Easter, and Whitsunday sermons *passim*.
[5] See *Serm. Justification* (v. 106 sqq.).   [6] *Opuscula posth.* p. 48.

ordained priest he had never ventured to discuss publicly or privately, or to preach on, predestination.[1]   In an age which prated of faith, he insisted that the value of faith lay, not in itself, but in its object and its moral issues and the effort it inspires : 'of itself it is but a bare act, faith ; a thing in-different: the virtue and the value of it is from the object it believeth in ; if that be right, all is right '[2] : 'neither fear, if it be fear alone, nor faith, if it be faith alone, is accepted of Him' :[3] 'we must not lie still, like lumps of flesh, laying all upon Christ's shoulders.'[4]   In an age of new ecclesiastical systems, he was content, and more than content, with the traditional system as he found it represented in the English Church, in so far as that was true to itself.

V

The purpose of recalling all this is to suggest what is likely to be found in the *Preces* and to indicate what is in fact found there and illustrate it by anticipation.

For the *Preces* are in a measure an autobiography.   In his prayers, Andrewes is real, actual, detailed.   He recounts, in thanksgiving and intercession, his circumstances and the conditions of his time : his devotion is brought to bear on his experience, and is marked by the absence of all vagueness and mere generality.   He commemorates his birth in the City, 'of honest parentage,' in soundness of mind, senses and limb, in 'competent state' and 'honest fortune,' so as in after life never to have occasion 'either to flatter or to borrow'; in 'times of peace,' such as it was in the middle of the 16th century; his baptism at All Hallows and his religious bringing up ; his two schools and 'gentle masters'; his College and the benefactors to whom he owed his educa-tion ; his 'attentive pupils' and 'likeminded colleagues,' 'sincere friends' and 'faithful servants,' and all who had been of use to him 'by their writings, sermons, conversations, examples, rebukes, injuries.'   He remembers an impressive event, like the earthquake of 1580 ; and to the end gives

[1] *Judgment of the Lambeth Articles* (*Cat. doct.* p. 294).
[2] *Serm. Pent.* xiii (iii 345) ; cf. *S. Giles' Lectt.* p. 544.
[3] *Serm. Pent.* xii (iii 337).
[4] *Serm. Tempt.* (v 483).

thanks and prays for all the cures and benefices he had held, and the souls who had been committed to his charge. And behind it all, he recalls his spiritual experience and his sense of the divine care and patience; his 'calling, recalling and further recalling manifold,' God's 'forbearance, longsuffering and long longsuffering, many times, many years.' [1]

And as the background of his own life, we catch sight of the large conditions of the world and the Church, the England and the Europe, the English Church and the Christendom, of his day. There is the Catholic Church and the unreclaimed world of 'pagans, Turks, Jews' beyond demanding her 'increase'; the long schism of East and West: the Eastern Church under the heel of the barbarian and crying for 'deliverance and reunion'; Western Christendom, torn and dislocated by the calamities of the 16th century, needing 'readjustment and pacification'; the British Church, 'keeping' indeed 'that which was committed to her, teaching the way of peace, maintaining,' in theory at least, 'order, stability and comeliness,' with 'pastors according to God's heart' as compared with those of the earlier years of Elizabeth; and yet not to be idealised, but all too imperfect in her attainment and wavering in her hold, and needing just the prayer for 'the restoration of the things that are wanting and the strengthening of the things that remain, which were ready to vanish away' [2]; a Christendom beset by the 'evils and troubles' which he probes and satirises and chastises in the Sermons—private interpretation, and innovation, the teaching of strange doctrine and doting about questions and making endless strifes, the dangers of heresies and schisms and scandals, of subservience to the civil power, indifference and contempt, arbitrary rule, robbery and simony and sacrilege, sectarianism and ignorance and the upstart pride of an unlearned clergy, and a meddling and censorious laity.[3] And in the civil sphere he has his eye on the commonwealths of the world and on his own, and their several estates and institutions; kings and lords and commons, magistrates, army and navy, education and commerce, farming, handicrafts, even the beggars. As an Englishman, we can see in him the glow of the pride and joy of the later years of

[1] Pp. 14, 61, 85 sq., 223 sqq., 272.
[2] Pp. 36, 60.   [3] Pp. 243, 268.

Elizabeth, in victory and peace, wealth and stability; the
development of trade and commerce and enterprise, and their
characteristic directions in the new husbandry, in grazing and
the fisheries.[1]   Perhaps he is too close to it to realise the
literary brilliancy of his age.   But along with his satisfaction,
there is the same sense of dangers as we find in the Sermons
—both the permanent dangers which beset all times, and
those which he could see illustrated at the moment whether
at home or abroad.   There is the danger of the adulation of
monarchs, of which he could see enough in the court of
James I, where he was himself an exception in his refusal to
flatter; and the peril to 'the temperance and holy simplicity
of the people' which came with the new wealth and pros-
perity.   And there are the political dangers and evils—the
'anarchy' of France, the 'tyranny' of Philip II, the foreign
domination which the Netherlands felt, and England dreaded
till the Armada was shattered; stupidity and secularity and
religious indifference on the part of rulers and legislators;
the corruption of justice, which the history of the fall of
Bacon shewed to be possible in the existing condition of the
courts; the policy of massacre and assassination, illustrated
by the Bartholomew and the Gunpowder Plot, the career of
Alva in the Netherlands, the attempts on Elizabeth's life,
and the murders of William the Silent and the Guises, and
the assassinations of Henry III and Henry IV of France;
the violence and licence and sacrilege of the military, illustrated in the Irish Wars and in the Thirty Years War of
which Andrewes lived to see the first 8 years; the strife of
parties which he could see everywhere; and the danger of a
failure of 'good and honest' men to fill high places and the
consequent accession of adventurers, of which perhaps he
recognised symptoms in the favouritism of James.[2]   And in
his repeated prayer for 'the speeding and reinforcement of
the Christian army against the enemies of our most holy
faith' and for 'our brethren in the galleys,'[3] we recognise
the peril of the Turks and their movements in Eastern
Europe and the Mediterranean, while no doubt he has also
the menace of Spain in view and the galley system of
European nations.

[1] Pp. 36, 49 sq., 60.   [2] Pp. 243, 246, 268.
[3] Pp. 50, 77, 92.

The three aspects of Andrewes' personality, as scholar, ecclesiastic, and saint, are reflected in his devotions.

1. In his sermon on the *Worshipping of Imaginations*, he reckons it among the vain imaginations, the 'idiolatries,' of contemporary puritanism, that it will not tolerate hearing any Latin or Greek, 'no, though it be interpreted,' nor 'anything alleged out of the Jews' Talmud,' 'but especially no heathen example or authority.'[1] The *Preces*, like the Sermons, are a protest against all this. For, first, they are written in a combination of Hebrew, Greek and Latin, the three tongues consecrated on the Cross. So far as can be judged, they were meant to be mainly in Greek ; at least the Latin was certainly in some cases, perhaps in all, only preliminary, while the Hebrew passages form but a small proportion of the whole. From what has been said above, about his use of Latin generally, and from the actual condition of the text as a whole, it would seem probable that Andrewes wrote his prayers for the most part first in Latin, even when their sources were Greek, and then turned them, or turned them back, into Greek, when he had shaped them into satisfactory form. The Hebrew is used in most cases, if not in all, only in quotations from Hebrew sources, and is sometimes, in Old Testament passages, only an accompaniment to the corresponding Greek of the Septuagint, defining more exactly its meaning. The greater part of the finished forms, as represented by the Laudian MS., is in Greek, even when the matter of them is derived from Latin or English sources, and the rest in Hebrew. Thus he recognises 'the cleft which God hath made in his Word,' which it is well to have 'in our tongues too' ; which 'hath still a necessary service, and maimed are we without it : for we must else receive the embassage from God by an interpreter, which is not so convenient.'[2] One of his editors has suggested that he chose Greek as his principal devotional language, not only for its sacred associations, but also for its wealth of compound words and its consequent force of expression.[3] His Greek is interesting and by no means commonplace ; but both in vocabulary and in grammar

---

[1] *Serm.* v p. 61.

[2] *Serm. Pentecost.* ii (iii p. 139).

[3] Hutton's Preface to Stanhope's version.

it sometimes leaves something to be desired in point of correctness; and in particular he shares with his contemporaries, the translators of the Authorised Version of the New Testament, a curious elementary defect in his inability to manage the combination of article, adjective and substantive, and seems unconscious that ὁ ἄνθρωπος ἀγαθός cannot mean 'the good man.'

Like much of the Sermons, the *Preces* are not original. In the whole mass of them there are comparatively few lines, perhaps none, that, considered apart, are wholly original: they are for the most part a mosaic of quotations. What has been said of Gray as a poet can be said, *mutatis mutandis*, of Andrewes as a devotional writer : ' Gray, if we may believe the commentators, has not an idea, scarcely an epithet, that he can call his own ' ; only the quotation must be continued —' and yet he is, in the best sense, one of the classics of English literature. He had exquisite felicity of choice; his dictionary had no vulgar word in it, no harsh one, but all culled from the luckiest moods of poets, and with a faint but delicious aroma of association; he had a perfect sense of sound, and one idea without which all poetic outfit (*si absit prudentia*) is of little avail—that of combination and arrangement, in short, of art.' [1]

The range of his materials and the use he makes of them, if it is inadequate to represent, yet suggests and illustrates, his learning. He seldom indicates the sources of his matter. The MSS. have a few original scriptural references; the greater part of the Harleian MS. gives the scriptural references with considerable fulness; and Drake has added a large number of references, one patristic, a few liturgical, the rest scriptural, in Wright's MS. Dr Lamphire gives a great many, mostly scriptural, in the Latin of the First Part; in the Second Part, the general indications of authors, sometimes misplaced, in the Reflexions on the several departments of devotion, seem to be original; but whether the references throughout the Second Part are original or are due to the editor cannot be determined. Later editors have dealt more fully with the scriptural sources; but no one seems to have attempted to trace the sources at all exhaustively. It is of course a task of some difficulty, and it must be more or less

[1] J. R. Lowell *My Study Windows*, 'Carlyle.'

a matter of accident, to distinguish them, nor is it always possible to say from which of two or more sources a given phrase or suggestion is in fact derived. But it is possible to indicate generally the range and character of the sources.

The first and principal source is Holy Scripture. For Andrewes devotion is the purpose of Holy Scripture. '*Thou hast magnified* 1. *thy Name and* 2. *thy Word above all things ;* 1. His Name, and 2. His Word. His Name for our invocation, his Word for our instruction. And these two, as they are the highest things in God's account, so are they to be in ours. Not the Word only, which carrieth all away in a manner in these days, but his Name also no less. For in the setting them down, the Holy Ghost giveth the first place to the Name. . . . And the very hearing of the Word itself is that we may call upon His Name. *How shall they call on* his Name *whom they have not heard ? How shall they hear without a preacher ?* So that preaching and hearing of the Word are both ordained for the calling on of this Name.' [1] Accordingly Andrewes uses the whole Scripture as a treasury of devotion. William Law has said, ' If [people] were to collect the best forms of devotion, to use themselves to transcribe the finest passages of Scripture-prayer ; if they were to collect the devotions, confessions, petitions, praises, resignations and thanksgivings which are scattered up and down in the Psalms and range them under proper heads as so much proper fuel for the flame of their own devotion ; if their minds were often thus employed, sometimes meditating upon them, sometimes getting them by heart and making them as habitual as their own thoughts, how fervently would they pray, who came thus prepared to prayer.' [2] This on a large scale was Andrewes' method, and it is likely that Law had the *Preces* in view when he wrote. Anyone who knows anything of the *Sermons* will recognise Andrewes' astonishing knowledge of the Bible, in its original texts and in its principal versions and in its minute details, and his spontaneity and dexterity in the use of it. And the same is observable in the devotions. In the Greek parts of them he uses of course the original of the New Testament ; and for the Old

[1] *Serm. Justification* (v 107).
[2] *Serious Call* xiv, quoted in this connexion by Dr A. Whyte in *Lancelot Andrewes* p. 34.

Testament he uses the Septuagint version, but here he frequently corrects the text by the Hebrew, or uses the Hebrew instead of or in addition to the Septuagint. In the Latin prayers, while his basis is the Vulgate, he habitually corrects it by the originals, or renders these anew, with or without reminiscences of the Vulgate in his mind. There is the same range of quotation as in the *Sermons*, the same imaginative skill in combination, the same appreciation of symbolical language, the same pregnant use of types. And in fact at times a commentary is needed to elucidate his meaning. Happily he generally supplies it somewhere in his other works; but sometimes it is impossible to be sure that one has caught his meaning or got to the bottom of an allusion, since his application of some passages seems to be determined by some ancient or mediæval comment on them or use of them. His quotations and allusions range over nearly all the books of the Bible: of the Old Testament all are used except perhaps Ruth, Obadiah, Nahum, Zephaniah and Haggai; of the Deutero-canonical books all but 1 and 2 (3 and 4) Esdras, the additions to Esther, Susannah, Bel, and the Maccabees—and here again he is making an implicit protest against the puritan 'imagination' that will tolerate no use of the Apocrypha;[1] of the New Testament he uses all the books except Philemon, and the 2nd and 3rd Epistles of S. John. The *Preces* point the way to a devotional concordance to the Bible; Andrewes develops whole subjects and turns them round, as it were, and observes them on all sides by collecting and arranging the allusions contained in the Holy Scriptures; he collects materials for whole departments and disposes them for meditation. And he thinks in terms of the Bible and its typical figures. The 'evils and difficulties' in Church and State alluded to above, are mostly recounted, not in abstract terms, but in the concrete form of the typical figures of Holy Scripture—Asshur, Jeroboam, Rehoboam and the rest.[2] And so it is elsewhere; like the *Sermons* the devotions are a study in the symbolism of the Bible; he delights in it and means something quite definite by it; it is no cover for vagueness or looseness of thought,

---

[1] *Serm. Worshipping of Imaginations* (v. 61).
[2] Below, pp. 243, 268.